Seeking Understanding

*Inspirational quotations
to bring clarity and comfort*

Lorna Arthur

Lorna Arthur works in a career information library where each day she meets people of all ages and religions who are seeking to build a meaningful life. She also spent six years teaching faith and values to teenagers at a Christian school in Perth.

Although Lorna was born and studied in England, she now lives in the capital city of Australia, Canberra. She enjoys writing and meeting new people, and is married with two teenage sons.

Her first book, **Rocky Road**, contains stories and parables about the Christian life. This and her books of inspirational quotations **Seeking God**, and **Seeking Courage**, can all be ordered through Autumn House.

First published in 2006
Copyright © 2006
Reprinted in 2008
All rights reserved. No part of this publication
may be reproduced in any form without prior
permission from the publisher.
British Library Cataloguing in Publication Data.
A catalogue record for this book is available
from the British Library.

ISBN 1-903921-36-8

Published by Autumn House
Grantham, England.
Printed in Thailand

Seeking Understanding

Inspirational quotations
to bring clarity and comfort

Lorna Arthur

Dedicated with much love to to our son Ashley

Seeking Understanding

Oh! the luxury of being understood!

Oh! the relief of finally understanding!

My human need to understand life has two sides, firstly I want to be understood and accepted, and secondly, I want to understand the world around me and find meaning in life.

This need for understanding is, in a sense, a quest for peace: world peace, and inner soul peace, something that all of us seek.

I hope the quotations in this small volume will help you to make more sense of God and of life, and bring you a greater sense of companionship and comfort as you too seek to be understood, and to understand.

Blessings!

Lorna

Bible references are brief paraphrases of the texts, so you can refer to the verses in your preferred version.

Understanding
God and faith

Midst of chaos

God,
Here in the midst of
life's chaos I stand,

Please guide me
and hold me
and take my hand.

Amen

God was there

In the beginning, long before human lips uttered the word 'psychology', or formed a perplexing question to ask, there was God, shaping man's mind from clay with his fingers.

God's dirty hands

God spoke all of creation into
existence, except for Adam and
Eve. For us he was willing to get
his hands dirty.

Different perspective

God says,
I know you find it hard to
understand me at times. You
and I just view things from
different perspectives. Don't let
this fact throw you off your
stride.
That's just how things are.

Isaiah 55:8-9.

Longing to believe

To wrestle with God is in the
time-honoured tradition of
honest seekers who, with all
their heart, mind and soul long
to believe.
Ask Jacob. Ask Israel.

Genesis 32:24–32

Like a fool

Whatever the current fashion
is for free speech,
if you say there's no God,
you're still acting like a fool.

Psalm 14:1

Pleased to meet you

When we are introduced to someone new we smile, shake hands, tell them our name and say 'Pleased to meet you', even before they have done anything for us. It is this kind of simple acknowledgement that God expects when we come to him. It naturally pleases him when we greet him openly, recognise his goodness and believe he has our best interests at heart. This, in essence, is faith.

Hebrews 11:6.

In the vastness

Am I afraid at times?
Of course I am.
Who wouldn't be?
I am just a smidgin of a
person in the vastness
of God's time and creation.
The only thing stronger than my
fear, is the knowledge of his
faithfulness.

God's desire

My ability to live with
unanswered questions is in
direct proportion to my belief in
God's desire, and ability, to save
me.

Job seeker

In a sense God is a 'Job Seeker',
and the Bible is his resumé.
Up until now, have you acted
like an interviewer who asks
awkward questions? The time
has come to decide whether to
take him on. What will you
choose to do? Search for a better
candidate,
one with more credentials?
Or will you give him the job of
being your Saviour?

Too heavy

Long before we were born he
knew that some things would be
too heavy for us to carry alone,
so he bore our griefs
and carried our sorrows.

Isaiah 53:4

God says, `Shine!'

We would like to shine for God
on warm sunny days, but often
we find ourselves surrounded
by the troubles of Earth's dark
night.
Yet even there, God asks us to
shine. To us this can seem both
unfair and impossible, until we
see how the moon, through no
light of its own, shines full and
bright in the darkness by
reflecting the light of the sun.

To empower us

It is said that
'absolute power
corrupts absolutely',
and that all human beings,
given the chance, would descend
into self-obsession.
Whether or not this is true,
the gospels portray a different
story. They tell us of a God who,
having absolute power, was
willing to give it away, in order
to empower us.

Through his spirit

Just as those who are truly
learned lay aside the parading
of their own wisdom to teach
others how to be wise, so God,
who had all power, laid it aside
to reach out to us and teach
and empower us through his
Spirit.

Over the line

When I am playing with sin, I
believe that I am alone, but like
an athlete at the Olympics I am
in Earth's stadium on the open
track and all of heaven is
watching my progress. They sigh
when I falter, hold their breath
when I stumble and, above all,
wait on the edge of their seats to
cheer me over the finish line.

Luke 15:7; Hebrews 12:1-2

Reconciled

We readily accept that the
Gospel urges us to be reconciled
to God, but if we read between
the lines
of the contract, we can see that
the deal also involves making
peace with ourselves, and
with our brother.

God's arms are long

Sometimes you and I act as if God was born handicapped, with short arms and deaf ears. But that is not the case; his arms are long enough to save you, wherever you are, and his ears can pick up your faintest whisper.

Isaiah 59:1-2

Focus!

I wonder if our expectations
and prayers have become media
driven, and our thoughts
started to focus more on things
than on faith. Do we pray for
today's lifestyle needs, then
become disappointed with God
when nothing happens?
Or are we still seeking and
finding the eternal life that
Jesus came to give?

Stop Playing

Come on, let's stop playing with
sin and grab our chance to talk
to God. Let's call him while he's
still within earshot by the door.
Quick, get a move on! This isn't
the time to drag our feet. This is
the time to act. The news is out
and I've heard it's true, he's just
itching to pardon us, and pour
out his mercy. Are you coming?

Isaiah 55:7

Strong tower

Like a mighty castle, or an ancient fortress besieged by tourists, is my God to me. I can run away from the crowds and hide in the strong tower of his mercy and love, and I am safe.

Psalm 91

Transformer

Is God against me,
and Jesus shielding me from
his power and wrath?
No way!
Rather, God has so much
power and love, that it
would overwhelm me,
so Jesus acts like
a transformer, bringing
the life and power to
a wattage that I can stand,
so I am able to light up.

No condemnation

Why do you think Jesus came?
Was it to condemn us?
Not at all.
That's far from true,
in fact he actually came
to save us from condemnation,
and give us abundant life.

John 3:17

True perfection

If perfection were the only goal
in life Jesus would have come to
earth to teach it, or even enforce
its pursuit. Instead he told us
that he had come to
'bind up the broken hearted'.
So to love and to heal are forms
of perfection after all.

Luke 4:18

He risked all

Consider this deep in your heart, and think it over often: God really loved the world. We know this because he was willing to risk everything to come here himself, in the person of his Son, so that anyone, anywhere on Earth who believed he was the Author of Life, would not have to die. He did this because he wanted us to experience, on a daily basis, what it felt like to have eternal life.

John 3:16

It really is finished

God knows, death does not
always come in peace. For some
people it comes violently or with
pain and humiliation. At such
times, we who look on cry out
from the depths of our souls 'It
is finished.' And in the days that
follow, when our souls lie prone
under the weight of deep grief,
the God of Easter whispers
through the darkness and tells
us that he
has been there before us, and is
even now, planning the
resurrection dawn.

Options

The gospels tell the story of two men who were disappointed with God, and were in despair over their own personal failures – Judas and Peter. One chose to turn in on himself, and die. The other took the risk of turning to God, even in the midst of his brokenness, weariness and confusion, and he was the one who lived. Lived fully and deeply, filled with the Spirit. The same options are available today.

Them and us

As soon as you say
'Our Father . . .'
you leave no room for
'them' and 'us'.
In all the world there are
only two types of people;
those who know they
are children of the Father,
and those who are yet to be told.

Light

Jesus said,

I AM the Light that shines on all
the people of the world, and
though not everyone has
understood the role of The
Light, no one has ever been able
to extinguish it, nor will they.

John 1:5-9

Understanding myself

Alone

There are times when we are alone, either in place or perspective, and we feel that we cannot safely share our burden with anyone else. It is then that we most stand in need of our own kindness and compassion.

Nature's message

In even the most humble and
rough brown bulb, nature packs
a message of beauty and hope
for the future.

Empty cup

Just as a cup can be empty of
water and waiting its turn in
the cupboard, so your soul can
be empty of courage and in need
of a rest. Just as you do not
worry about an empty cup, don't
worry about your empty soul,
for both can be refilled.

Don't be obsessed

Accept yourself, so that you do not need to become obsessed with self: your fears, your weight, your looks, your status. When self is a 'given' you can more readily enjoy the company of others and they can enjoy yours.

Heiress indeed

If I were an heiress, God knows,
I would have far more
confidence in my own worth.
I would hold my head high,
give and receive respect,
and look towards the future
with confidence. Turns out I am.

Ephesians 1:17-19

Goals

By his self-neglect the idealist says, 'I am nothing and the goal is everything,' so sooner or later he becomes too weary to achieve any goals. On the other hand, the realist says, 'To achieve anything I must be someone, so I will nurture my health and my sanity.'

From nothing

We often measure down from
perfection and come up short,
instead of measuring up from
nothing and seeing how blessed
and capable we are.

Today's life

Accept it, no age is perfect! Each age has its handicaps and opportunities; so just make the most of the age you are, and put your whole heart into living today.

Shaped for hope

We know that our past has shaped us, for better or for worse, and we are often willing to examine it in great detail to understand ourselves, but what we may not realise is that our view of the future shapes our attitudes and thoughts today just as surely. So ask questions of your future as well as your past, and live in hope.

Crisis

If you plan to live for eternity,
at what age do you have your
'mid-life' crisis?

Fuel

Hope for the future is the
fuel that fires up courageous
action today.

End in sight

Dark tunnels, by their very
nature, always come to an end.
You too will emerge into the
sunshine once again.

An act

Courage precedes peace.

Courage is an act of optimism.

Broken shell

Although it can be traumatic to feel your comfort zone being eroded and your comfortable shell breaking, it can be good news too, because it indicates that the shell you have been living in for so long has grown too small for the person you have become.

Focus, don't fear!

If your IQ is 100, and you use 10% on fear, and 10% on worrying about what other people will think, and another 10% on worrying whether you will fail, then you only bring 70% of your capacity to the task at hand. So it makes sense to use all your energy for focus, rather than fear.

Do and be

Some weeks are 'Do' weeks:
do the garage, do the lawn,
do the vacuuming.
Some weeks are simply 'Be'
weeks, 'I'll be there for you, and
you'll be there for me, and
together we'll make it through.'

The job

As a child, my identity was shaped by others, but now that I am an adult I have inherited the job.

Victim?

Self-pity is the shield I carry to deflect criticism, for if I can convince you that I am a victim in life you will expect less of me, and nothing will be my fault.

The first step

If you want to be understood by others, be willing to risk taking the first step, and explain yourself.

Make room

Sometimes you simply need
to cry out the sad
to make room for the glad.

Unshed tears

Sometimes a stomach ulcer is just an accumulation of unshed tears. Cry when you need to. It is good for your soul – and your stomach.

Self-obsessed

Even though you may feel weary
and sore, beware of becoming
too focused on yourself, because
those who are self-obsessed tend
to be thoughtless, and also
thought less of. A balanced life
cares for self and others.

No more reasons

Sometimes in the midst of our grief or pain, we don't need to hear any more reasons, we just want to rest our souls in kindness.

Help!

A man will fearlessly shout of his anger, yet fear to whisper the one word his soul is really crying, 'Help'.

Anger begins where power, control and hope end.

Independent

Help me, but do not make me
dependant on your help, or you
will not have helped me.
Instead, show me how I can
learn to be both independent
and resilient.

Just listen

Solitude teaches us
about ourselves,
if we are willing to listen.

Buried shame

There are times when we are restless and easily irritated by those around us. We strike out in anger and say things we will later regret. Often this is simply our own buried shame talking. What we most need, to heal our tempers, is the loving assurance that our own faults have been forgiven.

A breather

My mind can cope with life's changes more easily than my heart, so every once in a while I pause for a breather, to let my heart and soul catch up.

Like a lamb in spring

Jesus says,
Listen for my voice calling,
keep your ears open and stay
focused on me, then no one
will be able to snatch you away
from me or harm you, for I will
protect your soul, like the Good
Shepherd protects the
vulnerable new lambs in spring.

John 10:27-28

**Understanding our
relationships with others**

The best

Right or wrong, we all have this
in common, we each seek to do
the best we can from where we
are standing.

Climb the cliff

Encouraging words and kind
actions are like handholds and
footholds that help us climb up
the cliff of life.

Easy to carry

Kindness cannot always fix
things, but it can make life
bearable, for when two share the
laughter and tears, and the load
between them, things are easier
to carry. So even if you cannot
change things for your friend,
offer a listening ear and
proactive kindness.

Kind lift

It is easier to walk up a steep path when you are holding the hand of a friend.

To be kind is also to lift one's own spirits.

You will reap!

However smart you are, you can't fool God. It's simply a law of nature, that whatever you sow, you'll reap. This being the case,
we may as well sow kindness.

Galatians 6:7

Back door

If you are at odds with someone,
don't try by a superhuman
effort of your will to forgive
them and accept them anyway.
You will tear yourself in two.
Instead, use the energy of your
anger to try to understand
them, their fears, their motives,
their heart's longings. Then one
day, you will realise that hate
has slipped out of the back door
of your heart unheeded, and
compassion has entered.

Your **weakness**

You may have plenty of good reasons to criticise someone's behaviour, but don't get so full of yourself that you cease to recognise your own weaknesses. Keep humble, and simply give them a hand back up.

Galatians 6:1-3

Practise

If you must be a change
consultant, practise on
yourself first.

Matthew 7:2–4

Think differently

We treat people differently if we
believe they are acting from
sadness rather than badness.

Praise them!

If you have ten things to
criticise about a person, and you
can only find one thing to
praise, praise them quickly,
before the opportunity passes.

Don't crush – build!

If you use shame to make a
child obey, you will crush the
child's spirit and create self-
hatred and a desire for revenge.
Although in the short term
children may submit, in the long
run they will rebel. Instead
build into your children a sense
of
self-respect, and envelope them
with boundless and forgiving
love,
then they will catch a glimpse
of the grace of God.

Favour with God

Do you think you will find more favour with God if you put down your child to pick up a religious book?

Wide-eyed

In every adult, a wide-eyed child
either hides or thrives.

Relax

Tension arises when life's fears
are confined in the pressure
cooker of your apparent
helplessness. But however weak
you feel, you have more power
than you realise over your life
and your thoughts, so take hold
of that power and then, one by
one, release your fears, and
relax.

Melt fear away

You cannot reason, force or argue stubbornness, bred from fear, out of a person, but by showing them loving kindness you may be able to sneak a little warm assurance in, and then the fear will begin to melt.

Long fuses

People at peace with themselves
have much longer fuses when
dealing with others.

Sharp deal

At the other end of every sharp deal you make, is another one of God's children who has had a bad day. So, in every transaction, see the person before the bargain.

I'm a person

I do not enjoy being treated like a 'resource', I enjoy being treated like a person. The same is probably true of everyone you meet, including God.

Good reflection

When you enable another person to shine, it reflects well upon you.

Joy on the job

No matter how hard you try
you can never make another
person happy, nor can they
make you happy. When you
love someone you can try to
create an environment in
which love can thrive,
but joy is always an inside job.

Nurture

A man who is in love has no urge to kick his dog, likewise, a man who knows the love of God has no urge to criticise his brother, or belittle his wife or children, instead he nurtures them and cares for their feelings.

1 John 4:19-21

Grow

Working at a marriage often means working to grow beyond one's own selfish expectations and focusing instead on accepting one's self and one's life partner as they really are. Though the death of 'I want' may initially cause grief, it can give birth to the longed for joy of 'we will'.

Valued by God

If one person degrades another human being to a 'thing', making them sub-human, they can justify any behaviour. In this kind of situation, both lose power, respect and status. On the other hand, when we treat ourselves, and others, as valued children of God, everyone wins.

No difference

If you tolerate me it does not
mean that you like me, or even
think of me as an equal, it
merely shows that you want to
display your goodness and
benevolence
by putting up with me, for
tolerance is a second cousin to
prejudice. In contrast, love sees
no difference worth mentioning.

No Borders

Although humans draw national boundaries and launch missiles that cruise around seeking to make a mortal impact, God's Spirit knows no borders. Blithely ignoring politics and casting aside prejudice, his presence is revealed when a woman of one race shares a smile with a woman of another, where a man of one culture reaches out a hand to lift up a man in another, or where school children collect coins for books so that children of a different culture can learn to read in their own language.

Ingrate

Jealousy is ingratitude
with the sulks.

Teacher

Whether or not you
acknowledge it, you are a
qualified teacher,
it comes with being an adult.

Teach with laughter

By all means teach your
children to be resilient and
bounce
back from trouble, but also
teach them peace and joy,
by your own laughter.

Faster!

If you push things to go harder and faster, they go harder and faster, but if you push people to go harder and faster, they stop.

Stored words

If I carry a chip around on my shoulder from past slights, it stops me from hearing reason or praise, but amplifies even a whisper of criticism. Therefore, my challenge is, not only to listen to what people say, but also to learn how to dwell on the positive, and store kind words in my mind's memory bank.

Language of love

Lacking words, we use the short-hand of symbols to communicate our deepest feelings. We express nationhood by a bit of coloured cloth waving on the end of a flagpole; disinterest by lack of eye contact; romance and longing by giving a red flower with a prickly stem. Perhaps we would understand each other better if we studied each person's love language of encoding and de-coding, in school.

Love beauty

Can you appreciate a beautiful thing, without needing to possess it? Or get to know a friendly person, and enjoy their company without seeking to own them? If you can then you have learnt to love beauty and revel in kindness, but keep your soul free to create more of both.

His character

We've been almost bursting with joy and excitement, waiting to share with you what we experienced. Having him live here among us was just like meeting his Father in the flesh. He had a warm personality, and gave the same gracious answers that helped us to understand what was true. It really was like Father, like Son. How we wish you could have been here, and come to know the glory of his character face to face, for yourself.

John 1:14; 1 John 1:1-4

Rest

When my life speaks of God's
goodness and grace,
my lips can rest.

`Come and drink`

Jesus says,

You have travelled a long road,
often in the heat of earth's day.
You must be thirsty, thirsty of
body and soul. Come to me and
be refreshed, then you will find
yourself so alive in spirit, so full
of the essence of life, that it will
be like having rivers of life and
joy flowing from you to bless
others. *John 4:14*

Understanding Life

Time travel

However far you travel back in time, and whichever culture you visit, you will find that every emotion you feel today is common to being human. You are not alone, as you suppose, but in the good company of those who seek solutions, and find them.

Why me?

By all means, ask 'Why me?'
But to be fair, you will need to
ask it of everything you
experience: ask it of the clear
water gushing from your tap, of
the sun on your face and the
soft rain on your flowers. Ask it
of the bread on your table, and
the pillow beneath your head.
Most of all ask it of every good
relationship, and of the
abundant grace of God.

Law of life

Dear God,

Please teach me all I need to
know, to understand, what to do,
and to keep your law of life
and love in my heart.
David

Psalm 119:33-35

Confused?

Right now you may feel confused, but deep in your heart you already understand the principles that will lead you to answers.

You can sum them up like this: keep things simple, do whatever is right and just, enjoy being kind to folks whenever you can and keep on walking with God and humbly learning from him. Then, whatever religious fashions come and go, you will stay on track. *Micah 6:8*

Free gift

Peace is so prized that man will go to war to grasp it, only to find that the battlefront has moved from without to within. But there's no need for you to go to such extremes, because Jesus offers you inner peace as a free gift.

John 14:27

Solitude

Silence is the soul's temple and
solitude its place of worship.
Make friends with silence, for in
it you can both re-discover your
true self, and find healing from
God.

Power supply

So, you're not as young as you
used to be . . . so what?
Young men fall over and
teenagers sometimes trip up,
but those who come to me have
an eternal supply of spiritual
power at their command.

Isaiah 40:30-31

How to flourish

Just as too much lying in bed will give you bedsores, so going to religious extremes will aggravate your soul. Ignore fanaticism and live a balanced life, then you will flourish in body and soul.

Get on with it!

Procrastination is usually more tiring than doing the job itself because with your mind's eye you picture the job being done over and over, so you weary yourself out and still have nothing to show for it. It's a lot easier to do the job once.

Momentum

Overcoming inertia is like
pushing a car with a flat battery.
At first it is tough and slow
going, and you use all your
strength
to get the wheels rolling, but
soon you gain momentum and
the car then carries you.

Life poems

Even the smallest success, a line of prose, a line of washing blowing in the breeze, or a flower bed weeded, can help to lift you out of inertia. So, do not despise small beginnings, but see them as friends, because they bring you the gifts of self-respect and hope.

Shine out!

Come on now, its morning! Get up and let your light shine! Sure you can mumble and mutter in despair and hide under the darkness of the bedclothes, but why waste a good opportunity? My Spirit is right here ready to give you a new start and shine on your life, so what are you waiting for? Get up and make a difference. *Isaiah 60:1*

Layer by layer

I don't like adversity, nor apparently does the oyster. That is why, layer by layer, it transforms the grain of grit into a pearl.

The winner!

If reason tries to reason with
emotion, emotion will win.

Small boat, big sea

Fear of the waves is inversely proportional to the size of your boat, and the skill of your crew. Just as you have survived storms before, you can summon the tenacity to do it again.

Vocation

Whether you are seeking a life-long vocation, a career, or a part-time job, consider your own skills and needs, but also look at what problems in society need solving, then you're more likely to get paid on a long-term basis.

Want the job?

A potential employer is simply a person with a problem in one hand and a bag of money in the other. So, if you want the job, do some research and find out their problem, show them you would be the best person to fix it, then the wage is yours.

Prejudice blinds

An expectation is a form of pre-judgement that sometimes borders on prejudice. It can be as blind as love, and as temperamental. Tame your expectations of yourself, of others, and of God, before they rule and ruin your reality.

Dirty dishes

Temptation is a mental
taste test for sin.

Entertaining temptation
is expensive, and it leaves
lots of dirty dishes to clear
up in the morning.

Be set free

Lies and compromise have something in common with dirty dishes left on the sink; they multiply with time.

So, do not be afraid of the truth. When you know the most fundamental truth about who I am, you will ultimately be set free. *John 8:32*

`Time up!'

Worry is fear on a treadmill.

When we worry we command our fears to assemble, and urge them to speak up for themselves, uninterrupted by logic and uncensored by reason; unfortunately they usually oblige. In future, instead of letting them take over the conversation, have a mental bell that calls `time up', and refuse to listen further.

A fool at rest

Paul says,

As you've noticed, we're
still getting things wrong.
This made us feel like fools
and our natural instinct was to
wallow in our humiliation, and
let our failures drive us to
despair, but in the end we
decided to abandon false pride
and accept God's grace through
Jesus. That finally set our minds
at rest.

Romans chapters 7 and 8

Workman

Wisdom is knowledge with its
sleeves rolled up, and kindness
is grace in working clothes.

Sharp Tongue

Don't be fooled into thinking that a cynic is smarter than a believer just because they seem to be able to shoot everyone else's faith down in flames. A cynic is simply a quick-witted person who has developed a sharp tongue to defend their own heart from further pain and disappointment. Maybe you can show them where you found healing.

Sin ripples

Though kindness gives, it never
stands above another, though
kindness serves, it never grovels.
Kindness is everybody's equal.

There are as many ripples from
sin as from kindness. You alone
can choose.

Hold on!

Do you feel you can't cope?
That you're cracking
under the pressure?
Hold on!
After all, it's not God who has
given you this spirit of fear,
he's given you the gift of power,
of love and of a calm and
steady sanity. Grasp it.

2 Timothy 1:7

Into Joy

Whatever struggles you face
right now, whatever darkness,
the day will come when God will
lead you out of it into eternal
joy and peace. When that
happens you will be so filled
with happiness that laughter
will flow from deep in your
heart, and with sparkling eyes
you will look around at all his
creation and see it celebrating
right along with you.

Isaiah 55:12-13

Joyful

Go in peace,
knowing with a joyful heart
that Jesus is the Christ,
your Saviour.